Avoid being a Salem Witch!

Written by
Jim Pipe

Illustrated by
David Antram

Created and designed by
David Salariya

The Danger Zone

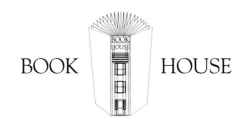

BOOK HOUSE

Contents

Introduction

Your name is Priscilla Bishop and your parents are innkeepers in Salem village, Massachusetts. The year is 1692 and these are troubled times. While you're afraid of being attacked by wild animals or Native Americans, your neighbours have an even greater fear – witches! When a group of local girls claim that someone has put a spell on them, a frenzied witch hunt begins.

You don't believe in witches, but many people at this time do, and your parents are arrested for practising witchcraft. For months your parents rot in a rat-infested prison, along with hundreds of others – while you and your brothers and sisters have to look after yourselves as best you can. Suspected witches are often tortured – and if you're found guilty, you'll be hanged!

In the 17th century, many people believe that witches are living all around them, doing the Devil's work.

Ouch!

Massachusetts Bay Colony

Salem

Boston

New York

NORTH AMERICA

Salem is part of Massachusetts Bay Colony in New England.

Strange goings-on

One night in January, during the bitterly cold winter of 1692, you overhear talk of strange events unfolding at the house of a local priest, the Reverend Samuel Parris. Parris arrived in Salem in 1688, with his wife Elizabeth, 6-year-old daughter Betty, 11-year old niece Abigail Williams, and his slaves Tituba and John Indian. Word is that Betty and Abigail are having fits, creeping under chairs, crawling along the floor and making bizarre noises. Even the village doctor, William Griggs, thinks it could be a witch's curse!

The fear of witches

The belief in witches was brought to America by settlers from Europe. There, for hundreds of years, innocent people have been accused of using evil spells to create storms, bring bad luck or make people ill.

MAGIC POWERS. Many people believe that so-called witches can change shape, fly in the night, and hurt people without touching them. They believe that witches keep pets, such as cats or toads, which are really demons in disguise.

EARLY DAYS. In 8th-century France, if you were suspected of being a witch your head was shaved and you were paraded around town on a donkey. If you were accused a second time, your tongue or nose was cut off. A third offence was punished by death.

Me? I never touched him!

THE WITCHES' HAMMER. In 1484, Pope Innocent VIII warned there was a real danger from witches. In 1486, two German priests wrote a book called *The Witches' Hammer*, a guidebook for witch hunters.

THE BURNING TIMES. From 1500 to 1660, witch hunts took place all over Europe. As many as 80,000 suspected witches – mostly women – were hunted down and punished by burning, hanging or strangling.

PINNED. When Ursula Kemp was hanged as a witch, her body was dipped in tar and put on show. She was then buried with spikes in her body to stop her rising from the dead. This was in England – where most people in Salem come from.

The Puritans

The Parris family are Puritans. Puritans are strict Christians who came to America to practise their faith in peace.* They work hard, pray a lot and live by very strict rules. Your parents' inn is a place where people drink and play games, so it is definitely *not* popular with the Puritans!

But rumour has it that young Betty Parris and her friends secretly enjoy fortune-telling games and magical stories told by Tituba, the family slave. Is she behind the fits?

*Salem *means* 'peace' in Hebrew.*

> That looks like fun.

Who wants to be a Puritan?

Puritan children must follow the same strict rules as their parents:

NO FUN! Puritans are not allowed to run, shout or play. Toys are banned. Playing with your friends in the village is strictly forbidden.

NO SLACKING! Girls help their mothers with housework and cooking. Boys have to learn carpentry, but they may go hunting and fishing.

Humpf... Idle hands do the Devil's work!

Handy hint

Don't miss church! In 1647 a man in New Haven fell into a river on Saturday evening. He missed church the next day as he waited for his only suit of clothes to dry. He was whipped for being lazy!

Gulp!

NO LIGHT READING. Puritans read few books other than the Bible. But some own books about evil spirits and witches that would give any child nightmares.

NO PASSION! In 1656 a Boston sailor was put in the stocks for two hours for kissing his wife in public after returning from three years at sea.

It was just a peck on the cheek!

The whole town's UNDER ATTACK!

Evil spirits?

Some people in Salem are convinced that a witch has sent evil spirits to attack Betty and Abigail. In other parts of America, people have been accused of causing failed harvests, bad weather and plagues. Your father is not convinced. He says that some folk are just looking for someone else to blame for their bad luck.

Things get worse when Abigail's friends Ann Putnam and Elizabeth Hubbard also begin to have fits. In February 1692, a neighbour, Mary Sibley, comes up with a plan. She tells Tituba, the Parrises' slave, to bake a so-called 'witch cake'.

A WITCH CAKE is made from rye meal mixed with urine from the affected person. It is then fed to a dog. If the dog starts acting strangely, this is supposed to prove that a witch has put a spell on the person.

Why me?

Tituba

10

Witch hunts in North America

Salem isn't the first place in America where there's been talk of witches. At least 100 settlers have already been punished for supposed witchcraft.

CONNECTICUT. In 1662, Ann Cole accuses Rebecca Greensmith of being in a witches' coven. Rebecca is hanged, along with her husband and at least two others.

BOSTON. In 1688, 13-year-old Martha Goodwin starts to have fits after a row with Irish neighbour Mary Glover. Soon after, Martha's brothers and sisters become deaf, dumb and blind. When witch hunter Cotton Mather investigates, Mary confesses she has bewitched the children, and is hanged.

Witch!

Witch yourself!

VIRGINIA. In 1698, Grace Sherwood is accused by a neighbour of turning into a black cat and attacking her. Grace is let off – but when another neighbour accuses her in 1704, she is given a witch's ducking. Plunged into deep water, she floats – a sign of guilt. But again she is spared the hangman's noose.

Now that's what I call a bad hair day!

Ducking stool

Handy hint

Get on well with your neighbours – or they might accuse you of witchcraft. Don't pick a fight or swear at anyone – some might think it is an evil spell!

A pox* upon your house!

*plague

RIVALS. Salem has two parts, a village and a town, about three hours' walk from each other. You live in the village. There are constant arguments between the poor villagers and the wealthier townspeople. When the girls begin to have fits, villagers accuse the townspeople of being witches.

'Rich' and 'witch' even sound alike!

11

Bewitched!

**B**y now, seven girls are having fits. One minute they writhe and choke, the next they go as stiff as a board. They also say they're being bitten and pinched by invisible forces. Many villagers really believe this is the Devil's work.

In late February 1692, Betty and Abigail claim that Tituba and two other local women, Sarah Good and Sarah Osborne, have bewitched them (put a spell on them). You suspect that the Puritan girls are just bored with their strict lives and are making up these stories to get some attention.

Who is a suspect?

Superstitious people believe witches have magical powers but look normal. However, they still have ways of spotting a witch:

GRUMPY? Sarah Osborne and Sarah Good are known for quarrelling with villagers. To some people, any woman who is grumpy, old, unattractive, unmarried or without children must be a witch.

OUTSIDER? Do you ever talk to yourself or dress eccentrically? Any behaviour that marks you out as being different can bring trouble. Some people suspect Tituba just because she is a Native American.

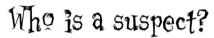

Oddball!

CHURCH MATTERS. Sarah Osborne hasn't been to church for a year. Is it because she's a witch? Last year some villagers tried to get rid of the Reverend Parris by refusing to pay his salary. His supporters may try to get their own back by accusing them of witchcraft.

They bewitched me!

Me too!

And me!

I'm not so sure, but I'd better join in.

Bonjour!

PARLEZ-VOUS? If you speak French, people might suspect you support the French raiders from Canada or the local Wabanaki people who have been attacking towns in the colony. Either way, you might be charged with being a witch.

SUCCESSFUL? In eastern Europe, courtiers often got rid of rivals by accusing their relatives of being witches. In Salem, too, people accused of witchcraft are often wealthy or powerful, like John Proctor and Captain John Alden.

A confession

On 1 March 1692, local judges Jonathan Corwin and John Hathorne begin to examine the accused. The meeting house is packed as hundreds of locals come to watch. The girls claim they were attacked by spirits sent by the three women. Other villagers blame the suspects for making their cheese go bad or making their animals sick. The two Sarahs deny being witches, but the minute they start talking, Betty and Abigail start to fit. This convinces everyone that they're guilty.

The girls also cry out when they see Tituba. Unlike the two Sarahs, Tituba admits to being a witch. There are others, she warns, and 'We all serve a master wizard.' It's a wise move on her part. Tituba is freed for confessing, though her claims only encourage other people to start suspecting their neighbours of witchcraft.

You little horrors! But if I don't confess I'll get beaten again.

WHY CONFESS?
Tituba confesses partly because she is beaten by Samuel Parris and partly because she knows that confessing will save her from facing trial.

What caused witch hunts?

TERROR. Many people in Salem are scared silly by Tituba's stories, especially when she says the witches are out to destroy Puritans throughout the colony.

REWARD. In England, 'Witchfinder General' Matthew Hopkins (below) executed more than 200 so-called witches before his death in 1647. His team earned £20 in just one visit – more than most people made in a year.

Handy hint

In some parts of Europe, you can spot witch hunters by the bags of salt that they wear as protection against evil spirits.

BELIEF. Puritan minister Cotton Mather (left) is a famous witch hunter. He doesn't take part in the Salem witch trials himself, but he's friends with three of the judges. He advises judge John Richards to force people to confess – even if it takes torture – and kill all who are found guilty.

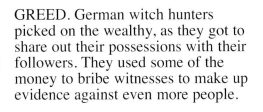

An army of devils is among us!

GREED. German witch hunters picked on the wealthy, as they got to share out their possessions with their followers. They used some of the money to bribe witnesses to make up evidence against even more people.

SCAPEGOATING. In 1580, the town of Trier in Germany was plagued by grasshoppers and mice. Two whole villages were blamed, and all were killed as witches. One judge who stood up for them was executed himself.

Accused!

The afflicted girls accuse more and more people. Ann Putnam is about to speak when her body goes limp. Suddenly she jumps up and lets out the strangest sound you've ever heard – half-bark and half-squawk. The judges ask, 'Who is tormenting you?' Ann is still for a moment. You're afraid she'll point at you!

On 21 April 1692 your mother and father are arrested, along with your mother's stepmother, Sarah Averill Wildes.

Think of the children!

What can you do if you're accused?

FLEE SALEM. Good idea – if you have time before you're arrested. John Alden, Elizabeth Cary and others escape from jail, mostly by bribing the guards.

We're all witches!

Honest!

CLAIM YOU'RE PREGNANT. This is called 'pleading your belly'. In law, women cannot be executed while they are still pregnant. The theory is that even if you deserve death, the baby inside you doesn't. If you try this, you'll have to hope that the witch hunt is over in 9 months!

CONFESS. Those who confess are not executed. Both Tituba and Abigail Hobbs escape death in this way. In all, 55 people admit to witchcraft in Salem. Of course, this makes even more people think the girls' stories are true.

16

The sheriff takes everything he can lay his hands on – furniture, beer, cows, pigs, sheep. Your 11 brothers and sisters are left behind to fend for themselves.

Handy hint

One of the easiest ways of getting out of Salem jail is to bribe the jailer. Well, that's easy enough if you're wealthy, but what if you're poor?

PLEAD INNOCENT. Actually, this is not such a good move. Nineteen innocent people try this and are sent to the gallows anyway.

FALL ILL. At first, 16-year-old Margaret Jacobs accuses others of witchcraft. When she decides to take back her evidence, she is accused of witchcraft herself. Luckily, Margaret falls ill and is unable to face trial – but she is imprisoned for another year until a kind stranger pays for her freedom.

ACCUSE SOMEONE ELSE. It's said that if you're a victim of witchcraft, you can't be a witch yourself. Some children even accuse their parents of being witches. But this doesn't always work. On 1 July your parents, Edward and Sarah Bishop, accuse another person, Mary Warren, of being a witch – but they are not freed.

You're a witch, Dad!

In prison

I n the town jail, the prisoners are crammed into a tiny, dark space with little food or water and no way to keep clean. The witch hunt soon spreads to nearby towns. By summer, 150 people are in jail awaiting trial.

In May 1692, town governor William Phipps sets up a special court in Salem. Five judges are appointed, including three friends of witch-hater Cotton Mather. They are led by William Stoughton, who already has a reputation as a ruthless witch hunter.

Cute little me, a demon?

But I'm a granny!

ANIMALS aren't safe either – two dogs are killed in Salem for being witches' demons, or 'familiars'. If you have a faithful dog or a bird that sings when it sees you, someone will think you're a witch – so hide your pet!

HISS!

Is no-one safe?

FORMER MINISTER of Salem George Burroughs is found guilty of being the witches' ringleader. On the scaffold he recites the Lord's Prayer perfectly – which is supposed to be impossible for a witch – but Mather persuades the crowd to hang him anyway.

Free him!

Hang him!

WOMEN. Rebecca Nurse, 71 years old and well respected in Salem, is found guilty. Then in April 1692, her sister Mary Easty is accused – a kind, religious woman with seven children. Perhaps some villagers just want to get their hands on her family's farm?

CHILDREN. Dorcas, daughter of Sarah Good, is put in jail. She is just 4 years old! The confused little girl confesses to owning a snake which sucks blood from her finger. Special baby chains are made for her and she is jailed for 8 months, until a neighbour pays for her to be freed.

TALL TALES. Even the most ridiculous claims are believed. Susanna Martin is accused of turning into a cat and trying to kill Robert Downer before flying out of the window. She is convicted and hanged on 19 July 1692.

18

The cells are damp, cold and infested with rats. Your legs are locked in heavy irons. It is thought that these chains will somehow stop your 'spectre' (ghost or spirit) from attacking others.

Handy hint

If you own an inn, get out of town! Bridget Bishop, John Proctor and your parents all run taverns. All are accused of witchcraft.

If any of you really are witches, now would be a good time to use your powers.

More than half the prisoners spend months in jail. At least four of them die there before being brought to trial.

19

On trial

In the gloom of the jail, Bridget Bishop shudders with fear. She will be the first to be tried tomorrow, 2 June. In court, Samuel Grey claims that Bridget's 'spectre' attacked him in the night. Eight days later, Bridget is hanged on Gallows Hill.

A month later, your mother and step-grandmother are put on trial. Your step-grandmother, Sarah Averill Wildes, refuses to confess. She is one of five women hanged on 19 July, along with Rebecca Nurse and Sarah Good. For the moment your mother escapes the noose. But she worries constantly about her children, forced to beg for food to stay alive.

What proof is there?

It's hard to defend yourself in a court that already believes you're guilty, especially when the so-called evidence is so bizarre. Cotton Mather urges the judges to take seriously the claims that people have been attacked by witches' spectres. How can anyone defend themselves against such outlandish claims?

TOUCHING TEST. The judges also decide to allow the 'touching test'. Accused witches are asked to touch their so-called victims. If they suddenly stop writhing, then people believe it proves that the accused is a witch and that the victim is under their control.

I haven't done anything!

WITCHES' MARKS. Bridget Bishop and others are poked and prodded to find so-called witches' marks – moles or warts that witches are said to use to feed blood to their 'familiars'. But most of us have moles somewhere on our body!

In England, witch hunter Matthew Hopkins stuck long pins into a suspect's body to test for witches' marks – enough to make anyone flinch!

Handy hint

Don't scoff at the girls' evidence. Deputy constable John Willard said they just wanted to get even with people they didn't like. He was accused of being a witch, and hanged.

Do I look familiar?

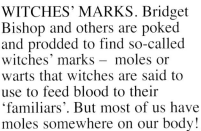

Judge Saltonstall's gavel

I quit!

NO DEFENCE. You can be accused by gossip alone and without real evidence. You aren't allowed a lawyer and you can't call witnesses. After the trial of Bridget Bishop, judge Nathaniel Saltonstall was so shocked by the unfairness of it that he resigned.

A FAMILIAR TRICK. Matthew Hopkins strapped his suspect to a chair and waited. If a mouse, fly or ant wandered into the room, he claimed the witch's 'familiar' had appeared.

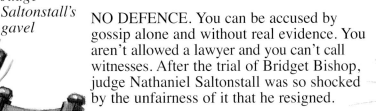

No mercy! She made my goat sick.

Hang her! She turned me into a skunk!

21

Crushed to death

Few dare to challenge the trials. John Proctor accuses the girls of faking their fits. Both he and his wife are jailed, and his children are tortured until they testify against their parents. On 19 August, Proctor is hanged with four others.

Old Giles Cory is accused of being a wizard but refuses to stand trial. The court allows him to be tortured, even though it is illegal. Cory is stripped and a board is placed on his chest. Heavy stones are then slowly piled on top of him. On 19 September, Cory dies when his ribcage collapses. His death at last makes people start to question the witch trials.

A world of pain

Giles Cory is not the only person tortured. Others have their bodies forced into hoops, with their necks roped to their feet. But the earlier witch hunters in Europe had even worse methods...

STRETCHED. European tortures included burning and dipping people in boiling oil, cutting off their skin, whipping, impaling them on spikes, or stretching their limbs on a rack (left).

BURNED. You remember Hansel and Gretel? Well, that's not just a fairy story. In Germany, suspected witches really were baked alive. In 1580, French witch hunter Jean Bodin wrote a book advising witch hunters to create new methods of torture and execution.

A wealthy farmer, Cory is a grumpy old man who often takes his neighbours to court. His main accuser is Ann Putnam.

Handy hint

Judges beware! Sarah Good's last words to Judge Noyes are: 'I am no more a witch than you are a wizard, and if you take away my life, God will give you blood to drink.' Noyes sent Good to the gallows, but died a few years later – choking on his own blood.

More weight!*

*Giles Cory's final words.

STABBED. An iron maiden is a torture machine with long, sharp spikes in the door that stab the victim when it is slammed shut.

Your confession sounds a bit fishy to me!

DREAD HERRING. In 16th-century Germany, victims were forced to eat salted herrings. This made them horribly thirsty. Then the torturers refused to give them water until they confessed.

Escape!

Scraping together their savings, your parents are able to buy their way out of jail. You all flee to New York. For you at least, the nightmare is over.

Three days after Giles Cory's death, on 22 September, eight more people are hanged. The trials have lasted all summer and now 200 people are in jail. The accusers are running out of local people to name. People begin to doubt the girls when they accuse Lady Phipps, the governor's very respectable wife. Now even Cotton Mather's father speaks out against the trials.

Witch crazes around the world

Witch crazes begin when one accusation leads to another. In Salem, Deliverance Hobbs accused others, including your step-grandmother Sarah Averill Wildes, to avoid being executed. It didn't save her.

WEATHER WATCH. At North Berwick in 1590, King James VI of Scotland personally supervised the torture of 70 people accused of witchcraft. Agnes Sampson confessed to sending a storm to drown King James while he was at sea. Euphemia MacCalzean hired lawyers to defend herself, but was burnt alive.

IN AUGUST 1692, your family escapes to New York. You stay there until the spring of 1693, when you move to Rehoboth, Massachusetts, to begin a new life.

Handy hint

Don't imagine you're safe just because you've fled Salem. By the end of the trials, more people have been accused of witchcraft in the nearby town of Andover.

IN THE PENDLE FOREST in England, 20 people were accused of practising magic and killing people with their familiar, a spotted dog. Nine-year old Jennet Device accused her granny, mother, sister and brother. Ten people were hanged. Jennet was hanged as a witch 20 years later.

IN FRANCE in 1676, Marie d'Aubray accused several well-known people before being beheaded as a witch for trying to poison her husband. A secret court known as the 'Burning Chamber' arrested 319 people, executing 36 and making many others galley slaves.

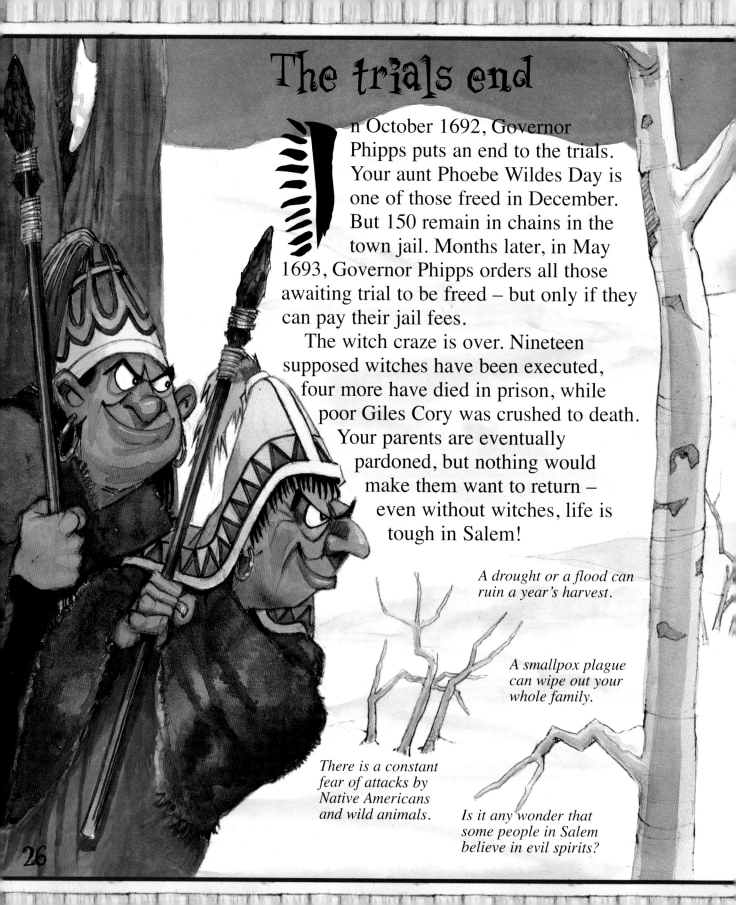

The trials end

In October 1692, Governor Phipps puts an end to the trials. Your aunt Phoebe Wildes Day is one of those freed in December. But 150 remain in chains in the town jail. Months later, in May 1693, Governor Phipps orders all those awaiting trial to be freed – but only if they can pay their jail fees.

The witch craze is over. Nineteen supposed witches have been executed, four more have died in prison, while poor Giles Cory was crushed to death. Your parents are eventually pardoned, but nothing would make them want to return – even without witches, life is tough in Salem!

A drought or a flood can ruin a year's harvest.

A smallpox plague can wipe out your whole family.

There is a constant fear of attacks by Native Americans and wild animals.

Is it any wonder that some people in Salem believe in evil spirits?

And I thought witches were scary!

Grrrr!

Handy hint

If someone accuses you, you can sue them for giving you a bad name. Several of the accused in Andover bring charges against their accusers.

Why did it happen?

SUPERSTITION? Belief in witches was widespread at this time. In Europe, tens of thousands of people had already been killed in witch hunts over the previous 200 years. If the adults in Salem hadn't taken the girls' stories seriously, the trials would never have happened.

BOREDOM? Some believe the girls' accusations of witchcraft were inspired by a mixture of stress, guilt and boredom.

GREED? Some families stood to gain property if the people they accused were found guilty.

POISON? One theory is that the girls were affected by a disease called ergotism. This can be caused by eating infected rye-bread. The disease causes violent fits, hallucinations, terrible itching and vomiting.

FAILURE? Anne Putnam claimed that George Burroughs had bewitched local soldiers during a failed raid against the Wabanaki tribe in 1688–1689. The judges in the trial led this raid, so perhaps it was convenient for them to blame the failure on witchcraft.

REVENGE? There was a feud between those who supported Samuel Parris and those who preferred former minister George Burroughs.

A fresh start

After the release of the suspects, a few people apologise for what has happened. But nothing can undo the harm done to the families of the accused. Hundreds of people with relatives in jail were forced to leave their farms and sell anything they could to pay the jail fees and travel long distances to visit their relatives. Your parents had all their animals and goods taken away. While in jail, they had to pay for their food and even their chains. Meanwhile, your brothers and sisters could have starved. But at least you survived the trials.

Your family has moved to the prosperous town of Rehoboth. But it takes 18 years – until October 1710 – before the courts declare that your parents and grandmother are innocent.

PLACING THE BLAME. In 1700, Boston merchant Robert Calef (right) wrote a book on the Salem witch trials. He accused Cotton Mather of stirring things up.

Where are they now?

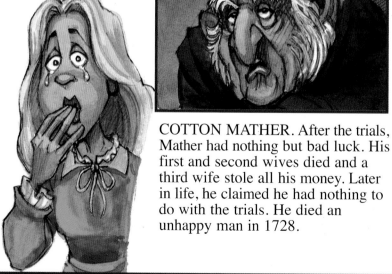

ANN PUTNAM. In 1706 she confessed to lying about the people she had accused, admitting 'Now I have just grounds and good reason to believe they were innocent persons.' She died at the age of 36.

COTTON MATHER. After the trials, Mather had nothing but bad luck. His first and second wives died and a third wife stole all his money. Later in life, he claimed he had nothing to do with the trials. He died an unhappy man in 1728.

TITUBA took back her confession. Her master Samuel Parris was so furious, he refused to pay the fee to get her out of prison. When she finally got out in spring 1693, Parris sold her to another family. Nothing more is known of her.

Handy hint

In Salem, anyone accused of being a witch has had their reputation ruined forever. Leaving town may be the best option.

The girls may have lied, but the people who believed them are as much to blame.

THE REVEREND SAMUEL PARRIS was replaced as minister of Salem village in 1697. He apologised to the people of Salem for his role in the witch trials. His niece Abigail Williams moved in with other relatives. When his wife died, Parris went to live in Boston with his daughter Betty and his son Noyes. He died a poor man in 1720 at the age of 67.

NATHANIEL CARY bribed a jailer to free his wife Elizabeth from prison. They fled to New York, but later returned to Massachusetts, where Nathaniel became a judge himself.

29

Glossary

Colony A settlement in one country that is loyal to and obeys the laws of another country.

Coven A group of witches.

Ducking A method used in the 16th and 17th centuries to decide whether a suspect was a witch. Suspects were plunged into deep water. If they floated, they were said to be witches. If they sank, they were deemed innocent.

Ergotism A disease caused by eating infected rye. Symptoms include violent fits, hallucinations, itching and vomiting.

Familiar An animal – often a dog, cat or toad – that was thought to be a demon or evil spirit controlled by a witch.

Feud A long-running quarrel between two families or groups of rivals.

Galley A ship driven by oars as well as sails. Prisoners were often forced to row in galleys as a punishment.

Gallows A wooden frame used for hanging criminals.

Gavel A small hammer used by a judge to call the court to attention.

Governor The person in charge of law and order in a village, town or state.

Hallucination An imaginary sight or sound.

Noose A loop of rope used to hang criminals.

Puritan A follower of the Puritan faith, a strict form of Christianity that arose during the 16th and 17th centuries.

Rack An instrument of torture on which victims were stretched by ropes.

Rye A type of grain that is turned into flour and used in baking.

Scaffold A platform on which criminals were executed.

Spectre A ghost or spirit. People believed witches could use their 'spectres' to attack victims without going near them.

Stocks A low wooden frame with holes for a criminal's head, hands or feet. Offenders were locked in the stocks as a punishment.

Testify To give evidence in court.

Touching test A method used in witch trials to decide whether the suspect was a witch. The suspect was made to touch the person who claimed to be bewitched. If the victim stopped writhing, the suspect was thought to be guilty.

Witch cake A cake made with the urine of a suspected victim of witchcraft. The cake was fed to a dog. If the dog started acting strangely, this was said to prove the victim was bewitched.

Witches' marks Sensitive marks or moles on the body, supposedly used by witches to feed blood to their 'familiars'.

31

Index